FINANCIAL REPORTING AND AUDITING IN SOVEREIGN OPERATIONS

TECHNICAL GUIDANCE NOTE

NOVEMBER 2022

ASIAN DEVELOPMENT BANK

CONTENTS

FIGURE

ABOUT THIS PUBLICATION

This guidance note is issued by the Procurement, Portfolio, and Financial Management Department (PPFD) of the Asian Development Bank (ADB) to assist ADB staff, consultants, and staff of executing and implementing agencies in preparing, presenting, and submitting audited financial statements for ADB-financed or ADB-administered projects.

 The following is a list of guidance materials on financial due diligence issued by PPFD, showing the phases in the ADB project cycle to which they apply.

| | Year Issued/ Updated | Processing | | | Implementation | Project Closing |
		Concept Stage	Fact-Finding	RRP	Reporting	PCR
Financial Reporting and Auditing in Sovereign Operations	2022	✓	✓	✓	✓	✓
Cost Estimation in Sovereign Operations	2022	✓	✓	✓	✓	✓
Financial Analysis and Evaluation	2019	✓	✓	✓	✓	✓
Financial Due Diligence for Financial Intermediaries	2018	✓	✓	✓	✗	✗
Financial Management Assessment	2015	✓	✓	✓	✗	✗
Guidance on Using the APFS Checklist	2015	✗	✗	✗	✓	✓

APFS = audited project financial statement, PCR = project completion report, RRP = report and recommendation of the President.

Source: Asian Development Bank.

Objective

This guidance note explains the requirements for presenting, auditing, submitting, and publicly disclosing financial reports for sovereign operations financed with ADB loans or grants or administered by ADB.

Living Document

This guidance note will be revised as needed. Various ADB policies and regulations (operations manual, project administration instructions) referred to in this guidance note are subject to revision from time to time. The reader is advised to consult the latest version of those documents.

The Reader

Readers are expected to use this guidance note to suit their needs. The reader is assumed to be a professional with basic financial knowledge, involved in activities supported wholly or partly by ADB-financed or ADB-administered sovereign operations.

FAQs

Frequently asked questions, clarifications, examples, additional information, links to training, and other useful resources are available on the ADB website.

Legal Concerns and Order of Priority

Legal agreements govern the legal relationship between borrowers and ADB. If there is any discrepancy between this guidance note and legal agreements, the legal agreements will prevail.

ACKNOWLEDGMENTS

This guidance note was drafted by a team of financial management staff under the guidance of Asian Development Bank (ADB) Chief Financial Management Officer, Aman Trana. The core team comprised Srinivasan Janardanam (principal financial management specialist), Akmal Nartayev (senior financial management specialist), Sajid Raza (financial management specialist), Maria Viviane Magno (associate financial management officer), and Aaron Pasquinel Cruz (associate financial management officer). Cecilia Peralta (senior financial management assistant), Jannine Cerilo (senior financial management assistant), and Teresita Contreras (associate financial management analyst) provided administrative support.

Copyediting was done by Hammed Bolotaolo, proofreading by Ma. Theresa Mercado, page proof checking by Marjorie Celis, cover design by Josef Ilumin, and layout by Rommel Marilla.

Detailed and helpful comments received during the interdepartmental review from ADB departments—Central and West Asia; Controller's; East Asia; Economic Research and Regional Cooperation; Independent Evaluation; Office of the General Counsel; Pacific; South Asia; Southeast Asia; Strategy, Policy, and Partnerships; and Sustainable Development and Climate Change—and from the various sector and thematic groups are gratefully acknowledged.

ABBREVIATIONS

ADB	–	Asian Development Bank
AEFS	–	audited entity financial statement
APFS	–	audited project financial statement
DMC	–	developing member country
FMAP	–	financial management action plan
IAASB	–	International Auditing and Assurance Standards Board
IFRS	–	International Financial Reporting Standards
INTOSAI	–	International Organization of Supreme Audit Institutions
IPSAS	–	International Public Sector Accounting Standards
ISA	–	International Standards on Auditing
ISAE	–	International Standards on Assurance Engagements
ISSAI	–	International Standards of Supreme Audit Institutions
MFF	–	multitranche financing facility
PAM	–	project administration manual
PFS	–	project financial statement
RBL	–	results-based lending
SAI	–	supreme audit institution
SOE	–	statement of expenditure
TOR	–	terms of reference

EXECUTIVE SUMMARY

The Agreement Establishing the Asian Development Bank (ADB), also known as the ADB Charter, requires ADB to "take the necessary measures to ensure that the proceeds of any loan made, guaranteed or participated in by the Bank are used only for the purposes for which the loan was granted and with due attention to considerations of economy and efficiency" (Article 14.11). The requirement for robust financial reporting, auditing, management, and monitoring of ADB sovereign operations is a critical component of ensuring that ADB operations comply with this mandate and contribute to the broader objectives of poverty reduction, inclusive economic growth, environmental sustainability, and regional integration.

Operational Priority 6 of ADB's Strategy 2030 mandates ADB to support its borrowers in strengthening their governance and capacity to plan, design, finance, and implement ADB projects. Strengthening governance through improved accountability and transparency ensures that ADB funds are used only for the purposes for which the loan was granted. Guided by sound banking principles, ADB promotes the implementation of international standards for presenting and auditing financial reports for sovereign operations financed with ADB loans.

ADB's requirements for financial reporting, auditing, management, and monitoring in sovereign operations are outlined in the Operations Manual Section J7. ADB requires that the borrower timely submits (i) audited project financial statements (APFSs) along with additional audit opinion on the use of loan proceeds and management letter for all loans; (ii) audited entity financial statements (AEFSs) and auditors' opinion on compliance with financial covenants in legal agreements, if applicable; and (iii) audited technical assistance financial statements for technical assistance projects delegated to the borrower for full or partial implementation.

Project financial reporting is required to cover total project expenditure from all sources of financing and reconcile funds received from ADB with ADB's financial data on loan disbursements. Borrower's AEFSs are required for submission to ADB when such financial statements are subject to audit under the statutory or regulatory requirements or where these are needed for project monitoring.

ADB requires the project financial statements (PFSs) to be audited by independent auditors whose qualifications, experience, and terms of reference are acceptable to ADB. APFSs are required to be submitted with (i) auditors' reasonable assurance opinion on PFSs, (ii) additional auditors' reasonable assurance opinions on the use of loan proceeds and compliance with financial covenants (where applicable) in the legal agreement(s), and (iii) management letter.

Timeliness is of the essence in financial reporting, and legal agreements require that APFSs be submitted to ADB for review annually within 6 months following the end of the borrower's fiscal year. ADB may agree to an exception to this requirement and extend the submission due date in the cases of decentralization where logistical considerations impact the physical flow of information.

The ADB review assesses the timeliness and quality of submitted financials and issues flagged by auditors (modification to the auditors' opinion, any material contained in the Emphasis of Matter paragraph, and/or issues identified in the management letter). Of particular concern are issues about the use of project funds. Upon review of the audit findings, ADB may request the borrower to prepare a time-bound action plan to address critical audit findings.

ADB financial management requirements are applicable for all financing modalities. ADB maintains the right to request audited financial statements for policy-based loans and policy components of sector development programs.

I.   Introduction

1.1   Strategy 2030 of the Asian Development Bank (ADB) guides ADB's efforts to eradicate extreme poverty and achieve its vision of a prosperous, inclusive, resilient, and sustainable Asia and the Pacific.[1] One of the seven operational priorities of Strategy 2030 is strengthening governance and institutional capacity in ADB's developing member countries (DMCs) to promote an enabling environment for sustainable growth.

1.2   Strengthening a borrower's governance and capacity to plan, design, finance, and implement ADB projects improves accountability and transparency. Guided by sound banking principles, ADB promotes the implementation of international standards for presenting and auditing financial reports for sovereign operations financed with ADB loans.[2] Such standards help ensure that the proceeds of any loan made, guaranteed, or participated in by ADB are used only for the purposes for which the loan was granted and comply with financial covenants incorporated in the legal agreements (footnote 2).

1.3   This guidance note applies to sovereign projects financed or administered by ADB through loans, grants, and technical assistance. It does not apply to policy-based loans (including the policy component of sector development programs), which provide budget support. Professional judgment must be exercised when preparing, presenting, and auditing financial statements as indicated in this guidance and applicable international standards. Appendix 1 contains a glossary of technical terms used in this guidance note.

1.4   This guidance note is intended to guide ADB staff, consultants, executing agencies, and implementing agencies in preparing, presenting, and timely submitting audited financial statements for ADB-financed or ADB-administered projects. The approach and methodology presented are based on ADB's operations manual and good international practice and, if consistently applied, should contribute to better governance.

---

[1]   ADB. 2018. *Strategy 2030: Achieving a Prosperous, Inclusive, Resilient, and Sustainable Asia and the Pacific*. Manila.
[2]   ADB. 1965. *Agreement Establishing the Asian Development Bank*. Manila.

II.   Overview of Financial Reporting and Auditing Requirements

A.   References to Operations Manual and Access to Information Policy

2.1   **Operations manual.** This guidance note is mainly based on Operations Manual Section J7 for financial reporting, auditing, management, and monitoring in sovereign operations, which requires the submission of the following:[3]

- audited project financial statements (APFSs) along with additional audit opinion on the use of loan proceeds and the management letter for all loans (excluding policy-based loans and policy component of sector development programs);[4]
- audited entity financial statements (AEFSs) and auditors' opinion on compliance with financial covenants in legal agreements, if applicable; and
- audited technical assistance financial statements for technical assistance projects delegated to the borrower for full or partial implementation.

2.2   **Public disclosure.** Public disclosure of the APFS, including the auditors' opinion, will be guided by requirements in the legal agreement(s) and ADB's *Access to Information Policy*.[5] The management letter and the additional auditors' opinions will not be disclosed.

B.   Borrower's and Auditors' Responsibilities

2.3   **Financial management arrangements.** The borrower is responsible for maintaining acceptable financial management arrangements and preparing the project financial statements (PFSs).[6] Financial management

---

[3]   ADB. 2022. Financial Reporting, Auditing, Management, and Monitoring in Sovereign Operations. *Operations Manual.* OM J7. Manila.

[4]   For results-based lending (RBL) for programs, the auditor should provide an opinion on the RBL program financial statements. A separate opinion on the use of loan proceeds will not be required.

[5]   ADB. 2018. *Access to Information Policy.* Manila. APFS and auditors' opinion on the APFS for technical assistance projects will not be publicly disclosed.

[6]   Financial management arrangements are evaluated during financial management assessment as outlined in ADB. 2015. *Technical Guidance Note on Financial Management Assessment.* Manila.

arrangements include project budgetary framework, external and internal audit, staffing, fund flow mechanism, financial accounting and reporting, management information systems, and internal control activities.

2.4   **Acceptability of financial management arrangements.** Acceptability of such arrangements depends on multiple factors and is ultimately assessed by ADB. Generally, financial management arrangements are considered acceptable if they (i) are based on sound internal controls validated by the borrower's internal auditor, (ii) have consistently applied agreed financial reporting standards, (iii) are capable of accurately and comprehensively recording all transactions and balances by financing source, (iv) facilitate the preparation of timely and reliable financial statements, (v) safeguard the assets, and (vi) are subject to independent audit. Acceptable financial management arrangements should be in place by loan approval (or earlier if the project entails retroactive financing) and be maintained up to the financial closing date.

2.5   **Financial management action plan.** If the financial management arrangements are assessed to be weak during processing, a time-bound financial management action plan (FMAP) to achieve acceptable financial management arrangements should be in place by loan approval. The project administration manual (PAM) should incorporate the FMAP.[7] ADB review missions should regularly assess the timely implementation of FMAP, and the borrower should report on FMAP implementation progress through periodic progress reports and/or annual project financial reports.

2.6   **Summary of auditors' and borrower's responsibilities.**
The responsibilities of the borrower and the auditor for financial statements, auditors' opinions, and management letter are summarized in the figure.

C.   Acceptable Standards

2.7   **Financial reporting standards.** ADB accepts PFS prepared in accordance with (i) International Financial Reporting Standards (IFRS) issued by the International Accounting Standards Board and the IFRS Foundation, (ii) International Public Sector Accounting Standards (IPSAS) promulgated by the IPSAS Board, or (iii) national equivalents. ADB accepts both cash- and accrual-based financial reporting prepared under acceptable standards. The basis adopted by the borrower for its entity financial reporting should preferably be adopted for project financial reporting to facilitate seamless integration of PFSs with the entity financial statements. However, if there is a reasonable justification for using a

---

[7]   Results-based loans have program implementation documents instead of a PAM. Multitranche financing facilities (MFF) have a facility administration manual, while MFF tranches have PAM.

Figure: Responsibilities of the Borrower and the Auditors

Activities	Borrower	Auditors
Preparation of PFS and management representation letter[a]	✓	✗
Independent audit of the PFS	✗	✓
Issuance of audit opinions (PFS, compliance with FC, and use of loan proceeds) and a management letter	✗	✓
Submission of APFS, auditors' opinions, and management letter to ADB[b]	✓	✗
Calculation of FC	✓	✗
Preparation of the auditors' TOR	✓	✗
Agreement on the timeline, including submission timing to ADB	✓	✓

ADB = Asian Development Bank, APFS = audited project financial statement, FC = financial covenants, PFS = project financial statement, TOR = terms of reference.

[a] International Standard on Auditing 580 deals with the auditors' responsibility to obtain written representations from management and, where appropriate, those charged with governance in an audit of financial statements.
[b] The borrower should arrange for the English translation of statements prepared in another language, preferably through the auditors or another translator.

Source: Asian Development Bank.

different basis (e.g., while the borrower follows an accrual basis, the project would adopt a cash basis), the PAM should describe such reasons.

2.8 **Auditing standards.** ADB recognizes the use of International Standards on Auditing (ISA) issued by the International Auditing and Assurance Standards Board (IAASB) and requires borrowers to engage auditors conforming to ISA. ADB also accepts (i) ISA-based International Standards of Supreme Audit Institutions (ISSAI) issued by the International Organization of Supreme Audit Institutions (INTOSAI), and (ii) national auditing standards when deemed sufficiently equivalent to ISA. Supplementary auditing and reporting procedures may be required if the national auditing standards do not conform to internationally accepted auditing standards.

2.9 **Equivalent national financial reporting and auditing standards.**
National financial reporting standards are considered equivalent to IFRS or IPSAS and are acceptable to ADB if their application results in sufficient and reliable financial information (including disclosures in the notes to the financial statements) that conforms in all material respects with the

form and substance of financial statements prepared using IFRS or IPSAS.[8] Assessing the acceptability of national financial reporting and auditing standards would usually be part of the existing country's public financial management assessments.[9] However, if such assessment does not exist or is outdated, the acceptability of national standards will be considered by ADB at the time of project processing.

2.10   A summary of ADB financial reporting and auditing requirements is provided in Appendix 2.

---

[8]   For instance, financial statements prepared under the Generally Accepted Accounting Principles in the United States are considered national equivalents of the international standards.
[9]   A common source of information is the World Bank's series of publications titled *Reports on the Observance of Standards and Codes: Accounting and Auditing.*

III. Financial Reporting Requirements

A. Project Financial Statements

3.1 **Project financial reporting.** Project financial reporting is required to

- cover total project expenditures from all sources of financing, irrespective of its eligibility for ADB financing (except cofinancing not administered by ADB);[10]
- reconcile funds received from ADB with ADB's financial data on loan disbursements every year during implementation;[11] and
- fully reconcile with ADB's disbursements at the time of the final APFS submission.

3.2 **Financial reporting language.** ADB requires the APFS to be presented in English for each financial reporting period.

3.3 **Financial reporting period.** The financial reporting must be annual, starting from the loan effectiveness date (or, if applicable, retroactive financing start date) and ending on the financial closing date (para. 3.11). The first financial reporting period will be from the loan effectiveness date (or, if applicable, retroactive financing start date, which is the date expenditures are incurred during the permitted retroactive financing period) till the end of the same financial year. Subsequent annual reporting periods will follow the borrower's financial year.

3.4 **Notes to the audited project financial statement.** The notes accompanying the financial statements shall provide sufficient information and explanations in narrative form or through appropriate tables, computations, schedules, and other information as stated in loan agreements and the PAM. Supplementary schedules may include details of inventories, long-term debts, accounts receivable and accounts payable, reconciliation with ADB disbursements, detailed disclosures on specific heads of project expenditure, and calculation of numerical financial covenants.

---

[10] In case of additional financing, if determined appropriate during financial due diligence, the PFSs for the original project and the additional financing should be combined.

[11] Project financial reporting during implementation should be on the same basis as adopted at the time of preparing project cost estimates to ensure comparability of the PFS with the project cost estimates in the report and recommendation of the President and the PAM.

3.5   **Audited project financial statement presentation.** The APFS will include information for current and previous financial reporting periods and cumulative figures from the project start date and be presented in the chosen currency (presentation currency). Presentation currency may differ from the currency of the primary economic environment in which the entity operates (functional currency). If the presentation currency is not the functional currency, it should be disclosed in the notes to the financial statements (i) the fact that the presentation currency is different from the functional currency, (ii) the functional currency, and (iii) the reason for using a different presentation currency as required by the applicable IFRS and IPSAS.[12]

3.6   **Reconciliation with ADB disbursement data.** The financial information in the APFS must be reconciled with ADB's disbursement records for every reporting period. The reconciliation statement should be included in the notes to the APFS and explain the reasons for discrepancies (if any) and describe the follow-up actions required (if any) to rectify the discrepancies with a timeline. Please refer to Appendix 3 for a sample reconciliation.

3.7   **Noncash transactions reporting.** The presentation of noncash transactions in the APFS would be in accordance with the financial reporting framework adopted by the borrower. Generally, if the cash basis of accounting is adopted, noncash transactions (e.g., land or other assets contributed by the government, exempt taxes, and duties) cannot be reflected in the APFS.[13] Instead, the estimated value of these transactions may be reported in notes to the financial statements. If the borrower adopts the accrual basis, a reconciliation between noncash transactions recorded in the financial statements and identified in-kind contributions in the cost tables included in the report and recommendation of the President or the PAM is recommended.

3.8   **Chart of accounts.** The adequacy of the borrower's chart of accounts to capture project-related financial data should be assessed during project processing.[14] If required, ADB should agree with the borrower to open additional "heads" (or subheads) of accounts to facilitate efficient project accounting and reporting. In addition, a mapping table needs to be prepared

---

[12]   International Accounting Standard 21 *The Effects of Changes in Foreign Exchange Rates* and International Public Sector Accounting Standard 4 *The Effects of Changes in Foreign Exchange Rates* provide a more detailed discussion on IFRS and IPSAS requirements on the use of presentation currency other than the functional currency.
[13]   However, any project-related counterpart cash transactions must be reflected in the project accounts as they would represent a cash inflow or outflow.
[14]   The objective of this assessment during the processing stage is to ensure that, during implementation, the financial information pertaining to the ADB-supported project can be identified and reported from the agency's financial reporting system. The project financial management staff should discuss and agree on this arrangement during processing. For details on the use of executing and/or implementing agency's accounting systems, please also refer to para 2.5 of ADB. 2022. *Cost Estimation in Sovereign Operations: Technical Guidance Note.* Manila.

(Appendix 4) and preferably attached to the PAM, linking different account heads in the chart of accounts with the PAM cost categories.[15]

3.9   **First and last audited project financial statement period.** A project's first financial reporting period may be shorter or longer than 12 months. The final reporting period may be shorter than 12 months (or longer if deferment of the final reporting period is allowed). Where the period between the previous fiscal year-end and the date up to which the final APFS is required (para. 3.11) does not exceed 6 months, the final APFS may cover a longer period of up to 18 months. In the interest of timely financial reporting, extensions longer than 18 months are not desirable.

3.10 **Final audited project financial statement.** The final APFS captures the total project cost incurred up to the loan closing date from all sources of financing and fully reconciles with the ADB disbursements as reported in ADB's financial records.[16]

3.11 **Final audited project financial statement period.** The period covered by the final APFS depends on the accounting basis adopted:

- **Accrual basis of accounting.** Expenditures up to the loan closing date should be included in the APFS for the period ending on this date, and no further APFS would be required.
- **Cash basis of accounting.** If expenditures are accounted for only when paid, the APFS will continue to be required until the financial closing date. However, if all expenditures are recognized as of the loan closing date, disclosed in the notes to the accounts as of the loan closing date, and audited, no further APFS would be required.

3.12 **Projects with more than one executing and/or implementing agency.** It is possible that one or more executing and/or implementing agencies physically complete the components allocated to them prior to the loan closing date, submit APFSs that are fully reconciled with ADB's financial records for their component(s), and have no further physical or financial activity. The APFSs submitted by those agencies for their respective component(s) will be treated as final, and they will not be required to submit APFSs during the remaining project implementation period.

---

[15] This is a dynamic process—the project team also has the flexibility to adjust ADB's cost categories to fit with the borrower's chart of accounts. The suggested mapping table will help the project teams better understand this issue.

[16] However, if the unreconciled difference between the APFS and ADB's financial data on loan disbursements does not exceed 1% of the ADB disbursements, or $100,000 (whichever is lower), the APFS may be accepted as final.

3.13   **Consolidation.** Consolidation of APFSs will follow applicable international or national accounting standards. IFRS and IPSAS permit consolidation only by a controlling entity that is controlling one or more entities.[17] APFSs of entities that are not under common control cannot be consolidated.[18] Each such entity should submit separate APFSs for the part of the project under its management, including a note with details of prorated allocation of financial charges. The borrower is responsible for obtaining the APFSs for all entities annually, compiling and aggregating the data, and reconciling them with ADB's records.

3.14   **Exception to the requirement of common control for consolidation.** A customized project implementation arrangement with common financial management arrangements (common chart of accounts, accounting, control, reporting, and auditing) may be established when executing and implementing agencies are not under a common controlling entity. In such cases, provided that the financial management arrangements, including auditors' terms of reference (TOR), are agreed upon and detailed in a project financial management manual approved in advance by ADB and all the executing and/or implementing agencies, PFS can be consolidated and a consolidated audit report and management letter provided by auditors.[19] The executing and implementing agencies should issue a joint annual management representation letter to the external auditors and authorize the auditors to have full access to the project documentation maintained by all agencies.

3.15   **Technical assistance delegated for full or partial implementation.** The borrower delegated to implement a technical assistance project shall maintain separate financial records for each technical assistance project and submit annual financial statements for the technical assistance following acceptable financial reporting standards.[20] Annual financial statements are required from the later of (i) the technical assistance effectiveness date, and (ii) the date of delegation; to the earlier of (i) the date when the delegated components were completed and all expenditures accounted for, and (ii) the technical assistance closing date such that they fully reconcile with the ADB disbursements reported in ADB's financial records. In cases where the total value of delegation is up to $1,500,000,

---

[17]   More detailed discussion on the requirements for consolidation can be found in IFRS 10 *Consolidated Financial Statements*, and IPSAS 35 *Consolidated Financial Statements*. Acceptable national accounting standards should have similar requirements for the consolidation of entities financial statements.

[18]   The definition of control requires professional judgment in each case. Financial reporting arrangements (including requirements for consolidation) should be defined during project processing while drafting PAM requirements for financial reporting and audit.

[19]   It is strongly recommended that the financial management, reporting, and auditing arrangements are agreed during project processing and incorporated in the PAM. However, in exceptional cases, if this were not done, they should be agreed before the preparation of the first APFS.

[20]   Instead of ADB, the recipient is accountable for technical assistance implementation and financial accountability. ADB and the recipient may agree on simplified financial reporting arrangements.

unaudited PFSs certified by the borrower should be submitted annually, and a consolidated APFS for the entire implementation period should be submitted at the end of the implementation of the delegated activities. If the total value of delegation exceeds $1,500,000, an annual APFS should be submitted.

3.16   **Harmonization with cofinanciers.** Where a project is cofinanced (except cofinancing not administered by ADB), all efforts should be made to harmonize the financial reporting and auditing requirements such that the borrower must submit only one set of APFSs and audit reports to all financiers. These harmonized requirements will be outlined in the PAM, including arrangements for sharing financial information between ADB and the cofinanciers. Where there is no agreement to harmonize the financial reporting and auditing requirements, the requirements for ADB's financial reporting and auditing will follow the guidance provided in the relevant operations manual sections, legal agreements, PAM, and this guidance note.

B.   Entity Financial Statements

3.17   **Audited entity financial statement requirement.** When an independent entity's financial statements are subject to audit under the DMC's statutory or regulatory requirements, or where these are required for project monitoring, such entity will submit to ADB the audited entity financial statement (AEFS) requirement in the English language. The financial statements should be prepared following the generally accepted accounting standards followed in the country or another standard if agreed upon during project processing. The entity's financial statements, together with the independent auditors' report, provide information on the financial governance of the entity and the environment in which the ADB-supported project will operate. In most cases, the legal agreement(s) would incorporate financial covenants based on the AEFS data.

3.18   **Incorporating audited project financial statement into audited entity financial statement.** While AEFSs are required to monitor the entity's financial projections, governance, and financial performance indicators that cannot be readily incorporated into PFSs, it is possible to incorporate APFS into AEFS in specific circumstances. In this case, the entity's financial statements, which reflect project-specific financial information, including auditors' reasonable assurance opinion on the use of funds and compliance with financial covenants (where applicable), are acceptable for submission, and there will be no need for a separate project audit opinion.[21]

---

[21]   Where PFSs are integrated with the entity's financial statements, the project components must be distinctly identifiable through disclosure or supplementary schedule detailing the sources and uses of funds of the project and other financial reporting statements. The management letter should cover project-specific deficiencies and weaknesses in internal controls and provide relevant recommendations.

C. Deadlines for Submitting the Audited Financial Statements

3.19   **Audited project financial statement.** Timeliness is of the essence in financial reporting, and legal agreements require that APFSs be submitted to ADB annually within 6 months following the end of the borrower's fiscal year. On an exceptional basis and with prior concurrence by ADB, this reporting deadline may be extended to up to 9 months from the borrower's fiscal year-end in cases of decentralization where logistical considerations impact the physical flow of information. During project processing, the financial management assessment will include the justification for extending the reporting deadline. In cases of limited capacity, the financial management action plan (FMAP) should include capacity development measures (to be implemented over the first 1–2 years of project implementation) to address the logistical constraints and enable the subsequent submission of the APFS within 6 months after the end of each fiscal year.

3.20   **Deferment.** APFSs are required for all projects for each fiscal year (including partial fiscal years), regardless of the size or number of financial transactions that occur within a fiscal year. In exceptional cases supported by sufficient justifications, the borrower may request for a deferment of the submission of the first or the subsequent APFS.[22] Deferment of the subsequent APFS may be requested only in cases of zero expenditure from all sources of financing in one or more fiscal years to be covered in the APFS concerned. In considering the deferment request, the benefits of a timely annual audit must be weighed against the risks arising from the delay with reference to the assessed financial management risk rating for the project and the borrower, the progress of an FMAP implementation, and the level of financial activity.[23] However, deferment of the APFS submission for cofinanced projects should be discussed with the Strategy, Policy, and Partnerships Department and/or Sustainable Development and Climate Change Department on the requirement for cofinanciers' consent.[24]

---

[22]   Only the APFS submission may be deferred, and the AEFS will continue to be required for each fiscal year from effectiveness to loan closing date. This is not a waiver, and the subsequent APFS should cover the deferred period. For example, if the first APFS is deferred, the next APFS still needs to cover the period starting with the effectiveness date (or the date when retroactive financing was incurred).

[23]   The cost of performing the annual audit is not an appropriate basis for concluding that the costs of the audit outweigh the benefits.

[24]   Some cofinanciers (e.g., the European Union) require ADB to provide an annual blanket assurance that funds have been utilized for intended purposes, for which timely availability of APFSs of all projects they cofinance is essential.

3.21   **Audited entity financial statement.** The project processing team should ascertain the legal requirements for the approval and disclosure of the AEFS for each entity and coordinate with the Office of the General Counsel to set the due date for the AEFS submission in the legal agreements. Since a fiscal year runs for 12 months, delays in the AEFS submission exceeding 12 months after the end of a fiscal year usually indicate weak financial management capacity and should be addressed. In cases where the entity implements more than one project, only one set of AEFS needs to be submitted to ADB with a cover letter referring to all the projects to which it applies.

3.22   **Disclosure.** Where an entity is required by law to publicly disclose its AEFS within a particular time frame, the legal agreements should adopt the same time frame for submission to ADB. In some jurisdictions, AEFSs must be submitted to or approved by an external authority at a particular time (e.g., the President of the country or the legislature) before they can be shared with other stakeholders. In such cases, AEFSs should be submitted to ADB within 1 month after the time limit for such submission to or approval by the relevant authority.

3.23   When applicable, the AEFS will be submitted to ADB annually for each fiscal year, starting with the fiscal year in which the loan was declared effective until the fiscal year in which the financial closing date falls or as may otherwise be stipulated in the legal agreements.[25]

---

[25]   The first AEFS will be for the first fiscal year that includes the date of loan effectiveness (or the date when retroactive financing was incurred, as applicable). The last AEFS will be required up to the loan closing date or financial closing date. If additional entities are included as implementing agencies during project implementation, the first AEFS for such entities should be submitted for the fiscal year when they are approved by ADB as implementing agencies.

IV. Project Auditing Requirements and Arrangements

A. ADB's Auditing Requirements

4.1 **Audited project financial statement submission.** Annual PFSs are required to be submitted with the following to ensure ADB is provided with reliable, comprehensive, and timely information:

- **auditors' reasonable assurance opinion** on whether the PFSs present fairly, in all material respects, or give a true and fair view of the project's financial position, its financial performance, and cash flows in accordance with applicable financial reporting standards;[26]
- **additional auditors' reasonable assurance opinions** on
  - use of loan proceeds to confirm whether the borrower has utilized the loan proceeds only for the purpose(s) for which the loan was granted, and
  - compliance with financial covenants (where applicable) in the legal agreement(s) to confirm the level of compliance for each financial covenant;[27] and
- **management letter** provided by auditors to communicate deficiencies and weaknesses in a company's organizational structure and internal controls, give recommendations on improving the internal control system, and update the status of implementation of prior period auditors' recommendations.

---

[26] ADB does not accept a limited assurance opinion or agreed-upon procedures audits.

[27] Auditors are expected to opine solely on financial covenants (for example, debt service coverage ratio, self-financing ratio, debt–equity ratio), in other words, only when the overall aspects of compliance related to accounting and financial matters are within the reasonable scope of auditors' professional competence. If the financial covenants pertain exclusively to the project, the project auditors may issue an opinion. If covenants are on enterprise-level financial performance, the enterprise auditor would be in a better position to provide an opinion. The financial management staff of the project processing team should discuss this requirement with the borrower's financial management staff and auditors and incorporate the requirement for an additional opinion into the auditors' TOR.

4.2   **Management representation letter.** Project management must issue a management representation letter to the auditor. The contents of such a letter would usually include affirmations that[28]

- the PFSs are free from material misstatements, including omissions and errors, and are fairly presented in accordance with the financial reporting framework acceptable to ADB;
- the borrower has utilized the proceeds of the loan only for the purpose(s) for which the loan was granted;
- the borrower complied (or did not comply or partially complied) with the financial covenants of the legal agreements (where applicable);[29]
- the advance fund procedure, where applicable, has been operated following ADB's *Loan Disbursement Handbook 2022*;[30]
- the statement of expenditure (SOE) procedure, where applicable, has been used following ADB's *Loan Disbursement Handbook 2022,* including the following: (i) appropriate original supporting documents substantiating the expenditure are available, (ii) the SOEs have been prepared following ADB's *Loan Disbursement Handbook 2022,* (iii) the expenditures stated in the SOEs comply with the approved project purpose and cost categories stipulated in the loan agreement, and (iv) the expenditures claimed in the SOEs comply with disbursement percentages stipulated in the loan agreement; and
- effective internal controls, including over the procurement process, were maintained.

B.   Auditing Arrangements

4.3   **Criteria for auditor selection.** ADB requires the PFS to be audited by independent auditors whose qualifications, experience, and TOR are acceptable to ADB. Both supreme audit institutions (SAIs) and private sector audit firms may audit ADB-financed projects. Auditors must satisfy the following criteria:

- Auditors must be objective and independent of the control of the entity or project to be audited and of the person or entity appointing them.
- Private sector auditors must comply with the local legislation, including holding relevant audit licenses/permits from the local audit regulator, if applicable.

---

[28]   Depending on the context, the auditor may request the management to provide other representations.
[29]   Considering the different timelines of APFS and AEFS submissions, this representation may be included in the management representation letter if, at the time of its writing, the AEFS has been finalized.
[30]   ADB. 2022. *Loan Disbursement Handbook 2022.* Manila.

- Auditors must conform to International Standards on Auditing (ISA).[31]
- Auditors must be well-established and reputable.
- Auditors must demonstrate experience in auditing financial statements of projects and entities comparable in type, nature, and complexity.
- Auditors must have personnel with the necessary capabilities to complete the audit competently and on time.

4.4   **Audits by supreme audit institutions.** Statutory requirements may mandate SAIs to conduct audits, where independence is usually assured under constitutional or legal provisions. If this is not the case, additional auditing arrangements may be required to remedy deficiencies. Where the SAIs subcontract project audits to private auditors, due care must be taken to ensure independence and that the private auditors meet the above criteria.

4.5   **Auditors' appointment period.** The borrower should preferably appoint independent auditors at or before the start of project activities and for each fiscal year until the issue of the final APFS. Auditors' appointment is recommended for the project period to ensure higher audit efficiency and reduce administrative costs.[32]

4.6   **Terms of reference.** The auditors' TOR prepared by the borrower will include the scope and details of the audit to be conducted, the various audit opinions required as specified in the legal agreement(s), and the timeline for submission. The TOR should preferably be agreed with ADB during project processing and included as an appendix to the PAM, and in any case, before the auditors' appointment. Appendix 5 provides a sample TOR that the borrowers may adapt to the project.[33] The TOR may also include other specific audit requirements that may be agreed upon between ADB and the borrower (e.g., performance audit, procurement audit, spot audit).

4.7   **Audit costs.** The costs of annual audits of PFS are included in the project cost estimates and are eligible for ADB financing.[34] Cofinanciers may request a separate audit of the PFS for the component(s) they finance. In such cases, the cost of annual audits of the external financing will be funded by the cofinanciers, whether as part of their contribution to the project or separately provided following the relevant cofinancing agreements.

---

[31] ADB also accepts (i) national auditing standards when deemed sufficiently equivalent to ISA, and (ii) the ISA-based ISSAI as issued by INTOSAI.

[32] This may be subject to any national requirements for auditor rotation.

[33] If ADB finances the cost of the audit, ADB is required to review the shortlisting criteria and the evaluation, as it is a project-funded procurement. For contracts not financed by the project, ADB can still support the SAI in developing the shortlisting criteria or reviewing the evaluation based on mutual agreement with the borrower and the SAI.

[34] For details on the final audit fee payment mechanism, when the audit fees are financed by ADB or through ADB-administered cofinancing, please see *Loan Disbursement Handbook 2022*, as amended from time to time.

4.8   **Financing audit costs claimed by supreme audit institutions.** In cases where the SAI audits the PFS and claims any fees or charges for such audit, such costs may be eligible for financing in line with either of the following considerations:

- The SAI has an established practice for billing auditees for services and overhead costs; in other words, they have regular charge-out rates, billing processes, procedures; etc.
- The SAI has engaged private audit firms or auditors to conduct the audit, which is considered an incremental cost associated with the audit.

V. Audit Reports Submission and Review

A. Auditors' Communication (the Audit Report)

5.1 Given the provisions of ADB's *Access to Information Policy*, 2018, it is recommended that auditors provide a separate stand-alone opinion on the PFS and separate opinion(s) for all additional requirements (para. 4.1 and footnote 4).

B. Auditors' Opinions

5.2 The auditors' opinion on the financial statements will specify the auditing standards followed in the conduct of the audit.

5.3 The reasonable assurance opinions on the (i) PFS, (ii) use of the loan proceeds, and (iii) compliance with financial covenants in legal agreements (if any) shall be governed by the ISA and International Standards on Assurance Engagements (ISAE) issued by the IAASB,[35] ISSAI issued by the INTOSAI,[36] or national equivalents.

5.4 The auditors' opinions will include, at a minimum, the following elements: (i) title, (ii) addressee (borrower), (iii) identification of the financial information audited, (iv) management's responsibility, (v) auditors' responsibility, (vi) expression of an opinion, (vii) auditors' signature, (viii) date of the auditors' report, and (ix) the auditors' address.

5.5 The auditors will pay particular attention to the following:

- The use of funds following the relevant legal and financing agreements;
- The provision of counterpart funds following the relevant agreements; and their use only for the purposes of the project for which the loan was granted;
- The maintenance of proper books and records that are reconciled with ADB's disbursement records;
- The existence of project fixed assets and relevant internal controls;

---

[35] IAASB. 2013. ISAE 3000 (Revised): *Assurance Engagements Other than Audits or Reviews of Historical Financial Information*. New York.
[36] INTOSAI. 2016. ISSAI 4000 (Revised): *Compliance Audit Standard*. Vienna.

- Where reasonable assurance has been provided using ISAE 3000 (Revised) or ISSAI 4000 (footnotes 35–36), the assurance report must contain, among others,
  - a statement that the engagement was performed following ISAE 3000 (Revised) or ISSAI 4000,
  - subject matter,
  - criteria for measurement,
  - a summary of the work performed, and
  - the auditors' conclusion;
- On the advance fund procedure (where applicable), audit procedures should be planned and performed to ensure (i) the advance account (including any subaccounts) has been managed following ADB's *Loan Disbursement Handbook 2022* (footnote 30), (ii) the cash balance of the advance account (and any subaccounts) is adequately substantiated, (iii) the expenditures paid from the advance account (and any subaccounts) comply with the approved project purpose and cost categories stipulated in the loan agreement, and (iv) the expenditures paid from the advance account (and any subaccounts) comply with the disbursement percentages stipulated in the loan agreement;
- On the SOE procedure (where applicable), audit procedures should be planned and performed to ensure (i) appropriate original supporting documents substantiating the expenditure are available, (ii) the SOEs have been prepared following ADB's *Loan Disbursement Handbook 2022*, (iii) the expenditures stated in the SOEs comply with the approved project purpose and cost categories stipulated in the loan agreement, and (iv) the expenditures claimed in the SOEs comply with disbursement percentages stipulated in the loan agreement; and
- Any weaknesses in internal controls over the procurement process.

C.   Management Letter

5.6   Financial statements audit includes assessing the internal control system relevant for preparing financial statements. The auditors may identify deficiencies in the internal control system during the assessment and the conduct of the audit, including irregularities in using ADB's advance fund procedures, SOE procedures, or the procurement process. The management letter indicates such deficiencies or weaknesses and recommends addressing them promptly. A management letter is provided to the authority charged with the project's governance. If no deficiencies or weaknesses are identified, the auditors should provide written confirmation that no management letter was issued.

D. Review Arrangements

5.7   **ADB review.** When reviewing audit submissions, the ADB reviewer will consider the (i) form and timeliness of the report; (ii) quality of the auditors' opinion; and (iii) audit scope, significant financial reporting policies, audit modifications, and other matters addressed by the auditors.

5.8   **Audit opinion.** The ADB reviewer will assess the implications of any modification to the auditors' opinion and/or any material contained in the Emphasis of Matter or Other Matter paragraph in the auditors' report. Of particular concern are issues about the use of project funds. Any modifications in the auditors' opinion will be reviewed and used to develop an action plan for future rectification.[37] Types of audit reports are discussed in Appendix 6.

5.9   **Management letter.** The ADB reviewer will examine the management letter and note any matters to which the auditors have drawn attention that may adversely affect project implementation, the borrower's operations, and the level of fiduciary risks to which the project and ADB are exposed. The review will note the borrower's response to the auditors' findings and any action taken to address the issue. In cases of failure to act or inadequate action taken by the borrower, ADB should elevate the issues to a higher level within the borrower and/or the government to address the situation.

F. Actions in the Case of Noncompliance

5.10   **Delay in audited project financial statement submission.** If the APFS is delayed by more than 6 months after the due date stipulated in the legal agreement(s), ADB will (i) withhold, with immediate effect, advances and replenishments to the advance fund, the processing of new reimbursement claims, and the issuance of new commitment letters; (ii) withhold, with immediate effect, approval of new contract awards for the agency in default; (iii) delay the negotiation or Board presentation of new loans where the agency in default is a participant; and (iv) deny extensions of the closing date for the agency in default.[38] Continued non-submission for 12 months after the due date may lead to suspension of the loan for the agency in default.

---

[37]   The project financial management staff should exercise professional judgment to assess the implications of modified audit opinions, take appropriate action, and engage in discussions with the borrower.

[38]   In exceptional circumstances, with appropriate justification, these consequences for noncompliance may be deferred by ADB for a specific period.

5.11   **Delay in audited entity financial statement submission.** For delays in submitting the AEFS and noncompliance in submitting the auditors' opinion on compliance with financial covenants, ADB shall pursue the matter with the borrower and the Ministry of Finance to achieve compliance.[39]

5.12   **Financial covenants.** Time-bound financial covenants in legal agreements are intended to protect and improve the borrower's financial sustainability.[40] Noncompliance with financial covenants triggers ADB's right to suspend the loan. However, ADB may decide not to immediately exercise its right to suspend. ADB and the borrower may first address the noncompliance through mutual discussions. Often, the noncompliance may be attributable to a failure to act by the government and/or a regulator (e.g., tariff revisions, equity and/or subsidy contributions, compensation for universal service obligations). In such cases, the project team should elevate the discussions to a higher level within the government. An FMAP supported by a detailed financial model may be proposed to recover from the consequences of noncompliance with financial covenants. The FMAP should provide (i) details, responsible entities, and deadlines for proposed measures; and (ii) the expected revised financial covenants compliance schedule.

---

[39]   Refer to para 3.21. Delay will be measured based on the submission deadline specified in legal agreements. In any case, AEFS submitted more than 12 months after the end of a fiscal year would indicate a weak financial management capacity, which needs to be addressed.

[40]   Noncompliance with a financial covenant in legal agreements will need to be dealt with in the same way as noncompliance with any other legal covenant.

VI. Reporting and Auditing Requirements and Arrangements for Other Modalities

A. Results-Based Lending Programs

6.1 Results-based lending (RBL) for programs may support the whole, part, or a time slice of a government-owned program by linking disbursements directly to the achievement of results. While ADB financing will be disbursed based on the achievement of results as measured by disbursement-linked indicators, the RBL program expenditure framework will be assessed to ensure that related costs are realistic and eligible for ADB financing. During processing, the project team should identify the total RBL program expenditure with reference to the specific account heads in the chart of accounts through which they will be accounted. If the ADB-financed RBL program is funding a part of the broader government program, it should be ensured that the chart of accounts has adequate capacity to distinguish between program expenditures within and outside the RBL program boundary. If required, the processing team should agree with the government on additional heads of account to be opened in the chart of accounts. The details should be incorporated into the program implementation document to serve as a guide during implementation.

6.2 The government finances RBL program expenditure from its resources, which may include, besides ADB loans, funding from other cofinanciers. All funds (including from the government, ADB, and cofinanciers) are commingled in the budget allocation for the program, and often the government will prefinance the program expenditure. Funds from ADB and ADB-administered cofinancing will be disbursed upon achievement of the results or identified as disbursement link indicators. As under RBL, ADB is not financing specific expenditures but rather the agreed results or disbursement link indicators; a separate audit of the ADB-financed portion of the RBL program is not feasible.

6.3 Unless universal procurement is approved for the program, the aggregate ADB financing for an RBL must be equal to, or less than, the aggregate eligible program expenditure incurred from ADB member countries.[41]

---

[41] If the amount of ADB financing disbursed exceeds the total amount of the government-owned program's expenditures (excluding expenditure pertaining to procurement from nonmember countries, unless universal procurement has been approved), after the winding-up period and final disbursement has been made, the borrower should refund the difference to ADB within 6 months after the RBL program completion date.

Annual and cumulative details of program expenditure, identifying the origin as either from an ADB member country or otherwise, should be provided as a note in the annual audited program financial statements. The auditors' TOR should include a requirement to assess the relevant arrangements.

6.4   The government will submit annual audited program financial statements to ADB within the agreed time frame as stipulated in the legal agreement(s).[42] Statutory requirements in many DMCs may mandate an audit by the country's SAI. There may be cases in which the audit reports from the SAI cover multiple projects or programs and do not provide sufficient details for the RBL program or are issued with significant delays. In such cases, during the processing of the RBL program, an agreement should be reached on the acceptable audit TOR to ensure that the audit of annual RBL program financial statements is conducted in a timely and acceptable manner. If the SAI is unable or unwilling to audit the RBL program, ADB and the borrower must agree on selecting an alternative auditor.

B.   Multitranche Financing Facility

6.5   Multitranche financing facilities (MFFs) finance investment programs that are implemented over a longer time frame than conventional investment projects. MFFs' financing is divided into two or more tranches, and each tranche may cover discrete investments, or all the tranches together may finance the same investment (time-sliced MFF). If each tranche of an MFF is for discrete investments, for financial reporting and auditing purposes, the tranches are treated the same way as stand-alone investment projects. Separate APFSs should be submitted for each tranche and should not be consolidated. For time-sliced MFFs, the APFSs for all the tranches may be consolidated, as they finance the same project (unless the executing and/or implementing agency is different for each tranche). Other requirements for submitting a management letter, opinions on using proceeds and compliance with financial covenants, and AEFS also apply.

---

[42] Since the ADB loan proceeds will be commingled with the government's resources, the auditor should provide an opinion on the RBL program financial statements. A separate opinion on the use of loan proceeds will not be required. The program fiduciary systems assessment should identify if the borrower's systems can track and record annual and cumulative details of program expenditure by identifying the origin as either from an ADB member country or otherwise as a specific note in the annual audited program financial statements.

C.   Financial Intermediation Loans

6.6   In financial intermediation loans, ADB usually finances credit lines for eligible subprojects through participating financial intermediaries. For financial intermediation loans,[43] an annual statement of the utilization of funds may be prepared instead of the APFS for financial reporting and auditing purposes.[44] Statement of utilization of funds may be considered as prepared under a special purpose framework, which is covered by ISA 800 (Revised), Special Considerations—Audits of Financial Statements Prepared in Accordance with Special Purpose Frameworks. The audited statement of utilization of funds may include

- statement of utilization of funds providing details, as indicated in Appendix 7;
- statement of budget vs. actual expenditures (any significant variance must be sufficiently explained in the notes);
- statement of advance account reconciliation for each advance account;
- statement of disbursement with a breakdown for each funding source; and
- detailed notes to the financial statements, including significant accounting policies.

6.7   Explanatory notes shall also accompany the audited statement of utilization of funds. These notes include the basis of preparation, significant accounting policies, reporting currency, undrawn external assistance, and details of sub-loans, such as amounts committed, disbursement up to the previous reporting period, disbursement during the current reporting period, cumulative disbursement, undisbursed commitments, percentage of loan utilized, etc.

---

[43] Or the financial intermediation component of loans that include more than one modality.
[44] If each financial intermediary were an independent entity, the statement of utilization of funds for each financial intermediary should be audited separately. The borrower, or project executing agency, should collate statements of utilization of funds from all independent financial intermediaries and reconcile them with ADB disbursements.

audited entity financial statement – the audited financial statements of the independent entity, comprising the financial statements, notes to the financial statements, and the auditors' opinion, including an opinion on compliance with financial covenants (if required) for each financial reporting period

audited project financial statement – the project financial statement along with auditors' opinion, a management letter, and additional opinions on the use of loan proceeds for each financial reporting period

auditing standards – the standards to be applied in the audit of the financial statements

auditors' opinion on compliance with financial covenants – a reasonable assurance opinion on compliance with financial covenants, supported by computations

borrower – in addition to borrowers of Asian Development Bank (ADB) loans and ADB-administered loans, it includes the executing and implementing agencies for the project and grant recipients, unless the context requires otherwise

delegated technical assistance – technical assistance delegated for partial or full implementation to an executing and/or implementing agency, whereby the executing and/or implementing agency is granted the authority to manage the technical assistance funds, make procurement decisions, and incur expenditure from the technical assistance funds

entity financial statements – the financial statements (including the notes to the financial statements) of an independent entity that are prepared following the financial reporting standards

final audited project financial statement – the audited project financial statement that captures the total project expenditure incurred to achieve the project objective and outputs from all sources, and is fully reconciled with ADB's financial data on loan disbursements

financial closing date – the date on which all project- or program-related financial transactions financed from the loan account are finalized, and the respective loan account is closed in ADB's books

financial reporting period (also referred to as fiscal year) – usually the 12-month period for which the borrower prepares its annual financial statements

financial reporting standards – a set of internationally comparable standards that are to be observed in the preparation and presentation of financial statements

functional currency – the currency of the primary economic environment in which the entity operates

general government sector unit – a government-owned or controlled unit that is primarily engaged in nonmarket operations (e.g., a government ministry and/or department, local government bodies)[1]

independent auditors' opinion – a reasonable assurance opinion provided by the independent auditors and other information that the auditors are required to provide in accordance with applicable auditing standards, through exercising professional judgment and the auditors' terms of reference, to those charged with the governance of the project and/or agency

independent entity – a nonmember borrower, executing agency, or implementing agency that has a legal identity separate from the government and operates to produce goods or services for the market but is not a general government sector unit

loan – includes Asian Development Fund grants and any loans and grants cofinanced from trust funds and other external sources and administered partly or entirely by ADB

loan closing date – the date on which ADB may terminate the right of the borrower to make withdrawals from the loan account as specified in the loan agreement

management letter – the formal communication from the auditors to those charged with governance and management of the borrower that highlights deficiencies in internal controls identified during the audit and proposes recommendations to address such deficiencies

management representation letter – a letter issued by the senior management of the entity being audited to the auditors, which states that all the information submitted is accurate and that all material information has been disclosed to the auditors. Through this letter, the senior management acknowledges that (i) they have fulfilled their collective responsibility for the preparation of the financial statements, (ii) they have approved them, (iii) the auditor has been provided with all relevant information and access as agreed in the terms of the audit

---

[1]   This classification is consistent with International Monetary Fund. 2014. *Government Finance Statistics Manual 2014*. Washington, DC.

engagement, and (iv) all transactions have been recorded and are reflected in the financial statements.

modified opinion – an auditor's qualified opinion, an adverse opinion, or a disclaimer of opinion

presentation currency – the currency in which financial statements are presented

project – project as defined in the legal agreement and covering the entire scope of the operation, from all sources of financing

project financial statements – financial statements of the project (including the notes to these financial statements) prepared following financial reporting standards acceptable to ADB to capture the total expenditure related to the project from all sources of financing. For financial intermediary loans, a statement of utilization of funds may be prepared in lieu of a project financial statement.

project management – refers to the project management unit, or the specific unit within the executing or implementing agency tasked with preparing, arranging, and timely submitting audited annual project financial statements to ADB

statement of utilization of funds – a special-purpose project financial statement of the project prepared in cases where loan funds are used for on-lending to eligible sub-borrowers through participating financial intermediaries

unmodified opinion – the opinion expressed by the auditor when the auditor concludes that the financial statements are prepared, in all material respects, in accordance with the applicable financial reporting framework

Description	Cash Basis of Accounting	Accrual Basis of Accounting
1. Project Financial Statements (PFS)		
1.1 Contents	Statement of cash receipts and payments Statement of budgeted vs. actual expenditures Statement of advance account (where applicable) Summary statement of expenditures (where applicable) Significant accounting policies and explanatory notes Any additional schedules (e.g., summary of assets, reconciliation with ADB's disbursement data)	Statement of financial position (balance sheet) Statement of financial performance (income statement) Statement of cash flows Statement of changes in net assets/equity/fund (where applicable) Statement of advance account (where applicable) Statement of budgeted vs. actual expenditures Summary statement of expenditures (where applicable) Significant accounting policies and explanatory notes Any additional schedules (e.g., reconciliation with ADB's disbursement data)
1.2 Relevant standards[a]	International Public Sector Accounting Standards (IPSAS): Financial Reporting under the Cash Basis of Accounting,[b] or national equivalent	IPSAS 1: Presentation of Financial Statements,[c] or IAS 1: Presentation of Financial Statements,[d] or national equivalent
1.3 Applicability	All sovereign funding modalities, except for policy-based lending (PBL) and financial intermediation loans	
2. Statement of Utilization of Funds (SOUF)		
2.1 Contents	SOUF comprising opening balance, name of financial intermediaries, details of sub-loans (committed lines of credit and amounts disbursed), closing balance, comparative figures for the prior year, cumulative amount to date Statement of budget vs. actual expenditures; any significant variance must be sufficiently explained in the notes to SOUF Statement of advance account reconciliation for each advance account Statement of disbursement with a breakdown for each funding source Detailed notes to the financial statements, including significant accounting policies	
2.2 Applicability	Financial intermediation loans	

continued on next page

Table A2 *continued*

Description	Cash Basis of Accounting	Accrual Basis of Accounting
3. Audit Opinions		
3.1 Overall opinion on PFS	Relevant Standards:[a] International Standard on Auditing (ISA) 700 (Revised): Forming an Opinion and Reporting on Financial Statements,[e] or ISA 705 (Revised): Modifications to the Opinion in the Independent Auditor's Report,[f] or national equivalent applicability (all sovereign lending modalities). SOUF may be considered as prepared under a special purpose framework covered by ISA 800 (Revised): Special Considerations—Audits of Financial Statements Prepared in Accordance with Special Purpose Frameworks.	
3.2 Opinion on the use of funds for the intended purpose	Relevant Standards:[a] ISA 3000 (Revised): Assurance Engagements other than Audits or Reviews of Historical Financial Information,[g] or International Standards of Supreme Audit Institutions (ISSAI) 4000 (Revised): Compliance Audit Standard,[h] or national equivalent Applicability: All sovereign lending modalities. ADB maintains the right to request audited financial statements for PBL and results-based lending (RBL)	
3.3 Opinion on compliance with financial covenants		
4. General Considerations		
4.1 Frequency	Annual (unless otherwise agreed with ADB)	
4.2 Submission timeline	Within 6 months of the end of each financial year—standard for all sovereign lending modalities, except PBL. Exceptions: in cases of decentralization where logistical considerations impact the physical flow of information, this reporting deadline may be extended up to 9 months from the fiscal year-end with prior ADB concurrence. An action plan to improve the financial reporting and auditing arrangements should be designed to ensure the submission deadline can be brought down to 6 months after the end of the fiscal year over a period of 1 to 2 years.	
4.3 Scope	Cover all financing sources, including ADB, counterpart, and cofinanciers, except cofinancing not administered by ADB	
4.4 Language	English (in the case presented in the developing member country's local language, the translation must be arranged by the executing or implementing agency, preferably through the auditors or a translator)	

[a] Relevant standards are for reference purposes only. These refer to applicable international standards at the time of this publication, which are subject to revisions and replacements from time to time.
[b] International Public Sector Accounting Standards Board (IPSASB). 2018. *Financial Reporting under the Cash Basis of Accounting.* New York.
[c] IPSASB. 2018. *IPSAS 1—Presentation of Financial Statements.* New York.
[d] International Accounting Standards Board. 2021. *IAS 1—Presentation of Financial Statements.* New York.
[e] International Auditing and Assurance Standards Board (IAASB). 2015. *International Standard on Auditing 700 (Revised): Forming an Opinion and Reporting on Financial Statements.* New York.
[f] IAASB. 2015. *International Standard on Auditing 705 (Revised): Modifications to the Opinion in the Independent Auditor's Report.* New York.
[g] IAASB. 2013. *ISAE 3000 (Revised): Assurance Engagements Other than Audits or Reviews of Historical Financial Information.* New York.
[h] INTOSAI. 2016. *ISSAI 4000 (Revised): Compliance Audit Standard.* Vienna.

Source: Asian Development Bank.

	Executing and/or Implementing Agency ($)			
Withdrawal application details	**Per project records/ APFS** (amount recorded in the PFS as reimbursement, direct payment, etc.)	**Per ADB disbursement information system**	**Difference**	**Remarks**
1				
2				
etc.				
Total (fiscal year to date)				
Total cumulative				

ADB = Asian Development Bank, APFS = audited project financial statement, PFS = project financial statement.

Source: Asian Development Bank.

Appendix 4: Sample Chart of Accounts Mapping Table

Account Code	Account Head
ADB PAM Cost Category – Civil Works	
A0001	Substation buildings
A0002	Transmission towers
A0003	Administration buildings
ADB PAM Cost Category – Consulting Services	
A0011	Consultants – transmission system
A0012	Consultants – distribution systems
ADB PAM Cost Category – Goods and Equipment	
A0021	Transformers
A0022	Transmission lines
A0023	Switchgear
A0024	Meters
ADB PAM Cost Category – Recurrent Costs	
A0031	Staff salaries
A0032	Office rental
A0033	Electricity
A0034	Heating
A0035	In-country travel
A0036	International travel
ADB PAM Cost Category – Financial Charges	
A0041	Interest and charges on ADB loans
A0042	Interest and charges on local currency loans
A0043	Guarantee fees to government

ADB = Asian Development Bank, PAM = project administration manual.

Source: Asian Development Bank.

Appendix 5: Auditors' Terms of Reference (Template)

A. Introduction

1. *[Describe the project with a focus on the purpose for which the funds are intended, consistent with broad project objectives and budget. Describe the executing and implementing agencies along with the related accounting and financial management practices, loan amount, financial reporting periods to be audited, and other relevant information that should be brought to the auditors' attention.]*

B. Management Responsibility for Preparing Project Financial Statements

2. Management is responsible for preparing and fairly presenting the project financial statements (PFSs) and maintaining sufficient internal controls to ensure that the financial statements are free from material misstatement, whether due to fraud or error. In addition, management is responsible for ensuring that funds were used only for the purpose(s) of the project; for compliance with financial covenants (where applicable); and for ensuring that effective internal controls, including over the procurement process, are maintained. In this regard, management must

   - prepare and sign the audited PFS, and
   - prepare and sign a management representation letter.

3. Management must include the following in the management representation letter:

   - that PFSs are free from material misstatements, including omissions and errors, and are fairly presented in accordance with the financial reporting framework acceptable to Asian Development Bank (ADB);
   - that the borrower has utilized the proceeds of the loan only for the purpose(s) for which the loan was granted;
   - that the borrower complied (or partially complied or did not comply) with the financial covenants of the legal agreement(s) (where applicable);
   - that the advance fund procedure, where applicable, has been operated in accordance with ADB's *Loan Disbursement Handbook 2022;*

- that the statement of expenditure (SOE) procedure, where applicable, has been used following ADB's *Loan Disbursement Handbook 2022*, including that (i) appropriate original supporting documents substantiating the expenditure are available, (ii) the SOEs have been prepared following ADB's *Loan Disbursement Handbook 2022*, (iii) the expenditures stated in the SOEs comply with the approved project purpose and cost categories stipulated in the loan agreement, and (iv) the expenditures claimed in the SOEs comply with disbursement percentages stipulated in the loan agreement; and
- that effective internal control, including over the procurement process, was maintained.

C. Objectives

4.   The objectives of the independent audit of the PFSs are to enable the auditors to provide (i) reasonable assurance opinions on whether the PFSs present fairly, in all material respects, or give a true and fair view of the project's financial position, financial performance, and cash flows; and (ii) additional opinions on the use of loan proceeds and compliance with financial covenants in legal agreement(s).

D. Auditing Standards

5.   The *[statutory]* audit must be conducted in accordance with *[specify the relevant auditing standards]*. These standards require that the auditors comply with ethical requirements and plan and perform the audit to obtain reasonable assurance about whether the PFSs are free from material misstatement. An audit involves performing procedures to obtain audit evidence about the amounts and disclosures in the PFS. The procedures selected depend on the auditors' judgment, including assessing the risks of material misstatement of the PFS, whether due to fraud or error. In making those risk assessments, the auditors consider the internal control relevant to the entity's preparation and fair presentation of the PFS to design audit procedures that are appropriate in the circumstances, but not to express an opinion on the effectiveness of the entity's internal control. An audit also includes evaluating the appropriateness of accounting policies used and the reasonableness of accounting estimates made by management and evaluating the overall presentation of the PFS.

6.   The standards to be applied will be recorded in the project or loan documents and will include (select one option):

> *Option A: Standards promulgated by the International Auditing and Assurance Standards Board (IAASB):*
>
> > *1.   International Standards on Auditing (ISA); and*
> > *2.   International Standards on Assurance Engagements (ISAE).*
>
> *Option B: Standards promulgated by the International Organization of Supreme Audit Institutions (INTOSAI):*
>
> > *1.   International Standards of Supreme Audit Institutions (ISSAI).*
>
> *Option C: National Auditing Standards:*
>
> > *1.   The auditing standards promulgated by [national authority].*

7.   While conducting the audit, the auditors will pay particular attention to the following standards:

- ISA 240/ISSAI 1240 – The Auditor's Responsibilities Relating to Fraud in an Audit of Financial Statements,
- ISA 250/ISSAI 1250 – Consideration of Laws and Regulations in an Audit of Financial Statements,
- ISA 260/ISSAI 1260 – Communication with Those Charged with Governance,
- ISA 265/ISSAI 1265 – Communicating Deficiencies in Internal Control to Those Charged with Governance and Management, and
- ISA 330/ISSAI 1330 – The Auditor's Responses to Assessed Risks.

E.   Project Financial Reporting Framework

8.   The auditors will verify that the PFSs have been prepared in accordance with *[International Financial Reporting Standards (IFRS) issued by the International Accounting Standards Board, or the International Public Sector Accounting Standards (IPSAS) promulgated by the IPSAS Board, or national equivalents].* The executing and/or implementing agency is responsible for preparing the PFS, not the auditors.

F.   Audit Deliverables

9.   **Audited project financial statement.** A reasonable assurance audit opinion on the PFS must be provided. The applicable financial reporting framework is a fair presentation framework.

10.   **Reasonable assurance opinion over the use of loan proceeds and compliance with financial covenants.** The auditors will provide a reasonable assurance opinion following *[ISAE 3000 Assurance Engagements Other than Audits or Reviews of Historical Financial Information or ISSAI 4000 Compliance Audit Standards]*

- that the proceeds of the loan were used only for the purpose(s) for which the loan was granted; and
- that the borrower or executing agency complied, partially complied, or did not comply with the financial covenants of the legal agreement(s), where applicable.[2]

11.   The auditors will outline the degree of compliance for each financial covenant in the loan agreement.

12.   **Management letter.** Auditors are required by ISA 260 to communicate audit matters of governance interest to those charged with governance. Accordingly, the auditors shall provide a management letter containing deficiencies or weaknesses in the internal control system during the assessment and the conduct of the audit, including irregularities in the use of ADB's advance fund procedures (where applicable), the SOE procedures (where applicable), or the procurement process. If no deficiencies or weaknesses are identified, written confirmation should be provided that no management letter was issued.

13.   **Specific considerations.** The auditors will, during the audit, pay particular attention to the following:

- The use of external funds in accordance with the relevant legal and financing agreements;
- The provision of counterpart funds in accordance with the relevant agreements and their use only for the purposes of the project for which the loan was granted;
- The maintenance of proper books and records;
- The existence of project fixed assets and internal controls related to that
- Where the audit report has been issued under ISA 800 or ISSAI 1800, it shall include the mandatory Emphasis of Matter paragraph alerting users of the audit report that the PFSs are prepared in accordance with

---

[2]   The borrower will provide detailed computations substantiating compliance with the financial covenants.

a special purpose framework and that, as a result, the PFS may not be suitable for another purpose;

- Where reasonable assurance has been provided using ISAE 3000 (Revised) or ISSAI 4000, the assurance report must contain, among others,
  - a statement that the engagement was performed in accordance with ISAE 3000 or ISSAI 4000,
  - subject matter,
  - criteria for measurement,
  - a summary of the work performed, and
  - the auditors' conclusion;
- On the advance fund procedure (where applicable), audit procedures are planned and performed to ensure (i) the advance account (including any subaccounts) has been managed in accordance with ADB's *Loan Disbursement Handbook 2022*, (ii) the cash balance of the advance account (and any subaccounts) is supported by evidence, (iii) the expenditures paid from the advance account (and any subaccounts) comply with the approved project purpose and cost categories stipulated in the loan agreement, and (iv) the expenditures paid from the advance account (and any subaccounts) comply with disbursement percentages stipulated in the loan agreement;
- On the SOE procedure (where applicable), audit procedures are planned and performed to ensure that (i) the SOEs have been prepared in accordance with ADB's *Loan Disbursement Handbook 2022*, (ii) the individual payments for expenditures stated in the SOE are supported by evidence, (iii) the expenditures stated in the SOEs comply with the approved project purpose and cost categories stipulated in the loan agreement, and (iv) the expenditures claimed in the SOEs comply with disbursement percentages stipulated in the loan agreement; and
- Any weaknesses in internal controls over the procurement process.

14. All reports must be presented in the English language within 6 months following the end of the fiscal year.

15. ADB's *Access to Information Policy* (2018) will guide public disclosure of the PFS, including the auditors' opinion on the audited PFS. After review, ADB will disclose the audited project financial statements (APFSs) and the auditors' opinion on the APFSs no later than 14 calendar days of ADB's confirmation of their acceptability by posting them on ADB's website. The management letter and the additional auditors' opinions will not be disclosed.[3]

---

[3] Such information generally falls under access to information policy exceptions to disclosure (ADB. 2018. *Access to Information Policy*. Manila. para. 17 [1–7]).

G. Other Matters

16. **Statement of access.** Auditors will have complete access, at all reasonable times, to all records and documents including books of account, legal agreement(s), bank records, invoices, and any other information associated with the project and deemed necessary by the auditors. The auditors will be provided with full cooperation by all employees of *[XYZ]* and the project implementing units, whose activities involve, or may be reflected in, the annual PFS. Furthermore, the auditors will be assured rights of access to banks and depositories, consultants, contractors, and other persons or firms hired by the employer.

17. **Independence.** The auditors will be impartial and independent from any aspects of management or financial interest in the entity or project under audit. In particular, the auditors should be independent of the control of the entity. During the period covered by the audit, the auditors should not be employed by, serve as directors for, or have any financial or close business relationship with the entity. The auditors should not have any close personal relationships with any senior participant in the management of the entity. The auditors must disclose any issues or relationships that might compromise their independence.

18. **Auditors' experience.** The auditors must be authorized to practice in the country and be capable of applying the agreed auditing standards. The auditors should have adequate staff with appropriate professional qualifications and suitable experience, including experience in auditing the accounts of projects or entities comparable in nature, size, and complexity to the project or entity whose audit they are to undertake. To this end, the auditors are required to provide the curriculum vitae (CV) of the personnel who will provide the opinions and reports, together with the CVs of managers, supervisors, and key personnel likely to be involved in the audit work. These CVs should include details of audits carried out by these staff, including ongoing assignments.

1. **Types of audit reports.** There are four types of auditor opinion reports:

    - Unqualified opinion (clean report)
    - Qualified opinion (qualified report)
    - Disclaimer of opinion (disclaimer report)
    - Adverse opinion (adverse audit report)

2. **Unqualified opinion.** An unqualified opinion is also referred to as a clean opinion. The auditor shall express an unqualified opinion when the auditor concludes that the financial statements are prepared, in all material respects, in accordance with the applicable financial reporting framework.[1] This report indicates that the auditors are fully satisfied with the company's financial reporting.

3. **Qualified opinion.** The auditor shall express a qualified opinion when

    - the auditor, having obtained sufficient appropriate audit evidence, concludes that misstatements, individually or in the aggregate, are material, but not pervasive, to the financial statements; or
    - the auditor is unable to obtain sufficient appropriate audit evidence on which to base the opinion, but the auditor concludes that the possible effects on the financial statements of undetected misstatements, if any, could be material but not pervasive.[2]

4. **Disclaimer of opinion.** The auditor shall disclaim an opinion when the auditor is unable to obtain sufficient appropriate audit evidence on which to base the opinion, and the auditor concludes that the possible effects on the financial statements of undetected misstatements, if any, could be both material and pervasive. In addition, the auditor shall disclaim an opinion when, in extremely rare circumstances involving multiple uncertainties, the auditor concludes that, notwithstanding having obtained sufficient appropriate audit evidence regarding each of the individual uncertainties,

---

[1] International Auditing and Assurance Standards Board (IAASB). 2015. *International Standard on Auditing 700 (Revised): Forming an Opinion and Reporting on Financial Statements.* New York.

[2] IAASB. 2015. *International Standard on Auditing 705 (Revised): Modifications to the Opinion in the Independent Auditor's Report.* New York.

it is not possible to form an opinion on the financial statements due to the potential interaction of the uncertainties and their possible cumulative effect on the financial statements (footnote 2).

5. **Adverse opinion.** The auditor shall express an adverse opinion when the auditor, having obtained sufficient appropriate audit evidence, concludes that misstatements, individually or in the aggregate, are both material and pervasive to the financial statements (footnote 2).

Annual Statement of Utilization of Funds for ------ For the Year Ended [dd/mm/yy] ([local currency])				
	Notes	Year 1	Year 2	Cumulative till Date
A. Opening Cash Advance		xx	xx	xx
I. Sources of funds				
1. ADB loan proceeds		xx	xx	xx
2. Others (e.g., repayments, interest earned)		xx	xx	xx
Total		xx	xx	xx
II. Utilization of funds				
1. Sub-loan(s) to beneficiary xx (with supporting schedule for details of on-lending) or beneficiary		xx	xx	xx
2. Sub-loan(s) to beneficiary xx (with supporting schedule for details of on-lending) or beneficiary		xx	xx	xx
Total		xx	xx	xx
B. Net Cash Activity (I - II)				
C. Ending Cash Balance (A - B)				
D. Cash in Bank				

Source: Asian Development Bank.

CPSIA information can be obtained
at www.ICGtesting.com
Printed in the USA
JSHW071113160523
41776JS00007B/223